DETTE KIM

Paperworks

Fun to make cards, models and mobiles

DAVID PORTEOUS
CHUDLEIGH DEVON

A CIP catalogue record for this book is
available from the British Library.

Published by David Porteous
PO Box 5
Chudleigh
Newton Abbot
Devon TQ13 0YZ

ISBN 0 870586 04 2

Translated by Tim Bowler

Printed in Singapore

CONTENTS

INTRODUCTION

This book will show you how, with simple materials, a little dexterity and patience, and a good deal of imagination, you can turn a piece of flat paper or card into a three-dimensional 'work of art'. Some of the instructions in the book can be carried out quickly; others require a little more patience and precision. But paper and card are comparatively cheap materials, so even if you are not successful first time, the damage should not be too great.

It is my hope that the models in this book will inspire young and old alike, for papercrafts are not limited to any particular age group. All the models are illustrated in colour to enable you to see the finished product. Alongside each heading you will see a number in brackets. This indicates the page on which you will find a colour picture of that particular model.

Pages 10–13 give a number of practical hints and describe the equipment you will need. If you read these pages before you start to make the models you should find the answers to many of the problems that you are likely to meet along the way.

So, get snipping and have fun!

Dette Kim

HOW TO FOLD

Many of the models in this book, for example the animals on pages 14–31, are made by folding paper or card. For the best results it is important to make sure that the folds are absolutely sharp and clear. For that reason it is a good idea to scratch a line with a blunt needle along a ruler before you fold. But make sure you do not scratch so hard that the needle goes through the paper or card. The fold-lines on the templates are marked with two different kinds of dotted line:

– – – – means a mountain fold (fold up).
.... means a valley fold (fold down).

When you transfer the templates to the card or paper draw in the fold lines with a pencil so that they can be erased later. The illustrations below show a few examples of valley and mountain folds.

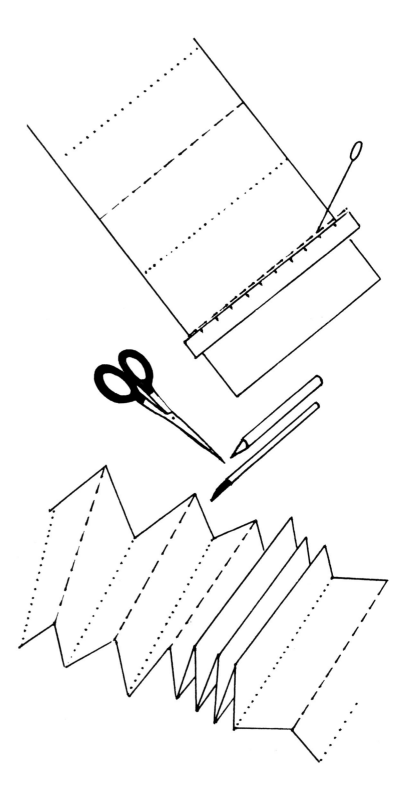

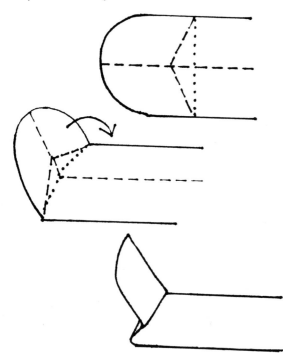

TEMPLATES

All the templates in this book are drawn to full size on a grid with squares of 1x1 cm. This grid makes it easier to copy a template and, if necessary, to produce an enlargement. If you want to copy a template at twice the size draw a grid with the same number of squares as the original but in the new grid the squares should be 2x2 cm. First choose a starting-point on the template drawing, then find the corresponding square on the grid you have plotted. Mark the points where the line crosses the edge of the square. Join the two points with a line as on the template drawing. Now you can draw the template square by square.

If you want to use the template in its original size you can also draw it on tracing paper or photocopy it. Then transfer the template to the paper or card with the help of carbon paper.

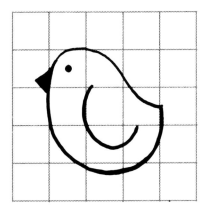

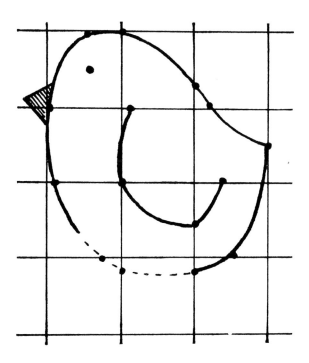

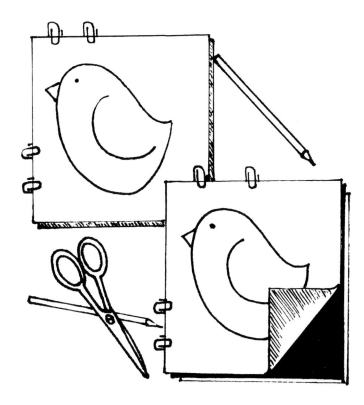

TOOLS AND MATERIALS

You must use the proper tools and materials if you are to achieve pleasing results. This section gives you some information on the basic equipment you will need.

Pencil: Whether you are drawing on cardboard or paper it is best to use a soft pencil. That way you can rub out the line if you make a mistake.

Stapler: You can often use a stapler instead of glue, but only when the staples will not show.

Craft knife: A craft knife is sometimes easier to use than a pair of scissors. The best knives are those with the blades inside the shaft which can be broken off as they become blunt. You can also use a scalpel. But be very careful: both tools can be dangerous!

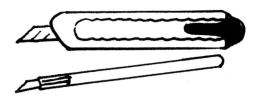

Punch pliers: Punch pliers or a hole punch can be used for cutting eyes.

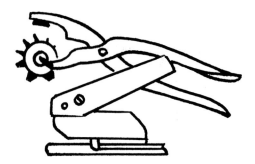

Carbon paper: Use carbon paper to transfer a drawing or template from one piece of paper to another. Never transfer the model directly from the book. Draw the template onto tracing paper or use a photocopier. Alternatively use the grid method described on page 11.

Card: Many different colours and grades of card are used for the models in this book. Craft and art shops stock a wide range, and you can practise on old greetings cards.

Photocopying machine: A photocopying machine is useful if you want to transfer a template quickly to a piece of paper or thin card. Some machines can also reduce and enlarge. When the template has been copied it can be transferred to the card or paper using carbon paper.

Glue-stick: A glue-stick is easy to work with, especially for small children. You can also use a PVA glue.

Ruler: You can use a ruler for measuring. A steel-edged ruler is handy for cutting along.

Paper: Coloured paper has been used for many of the models. You could, for example, try origami paper, which is coloured on both sides, or scraps of gift wrap.

Paper-clips: Paper-clips are ideal for holding two glued surfaces together while they are drying. You can also use small bulldog clips.

A pair of compasses: A pair of compasses is extremely helpful for drawing circles.

Tracing paper: See carbon paper.

Tweezers: Tweezers are very useful, for example, when you need to press small folds into position or to glue eyes in place.

Scissors: A pair of narrow-tipped paper scissors is one of the most important items you will need.

Scalpel: See craft knife.

Cutting base: For a base you could, if necessary, make do with a sturdy piece of cardboard, but it is better to use a special rubber base, such as you can buy in craft shops.

Needle: Use a blunt needle for scratching fold-lines; see page 10.

Felt pen: A felt pen is useful for drawing eyes, facial features and patterns.

Rubber: A rubber can be helpful when you want to erase fold-lines.

13

14

CATS [17]

The cats can be cut from thin card or paper. Fold the paper or card in two. Transfer the template so that the dotted line matches the fold. Cut out the figure. Cut the mouth out through both layers. Make slits for the whiskers as shown in the illustration below. Fold the cat along the dotted lines.

Cut or trim the whiskers from thin white paper. They should be about 3 cm long and 1 mm wide. Push the whiskers through the slits as shown below.

Nose, eyes and any stripes or spots can be added with a felt pen. You can also cut out a bow tie and glue it on both sides of the neck.

The fish can be cut and folded from thin paper.

Dog, pages 18–20.

Dogs, pages 18–20. Kennel, page 21.

Cats, pages 14–15.

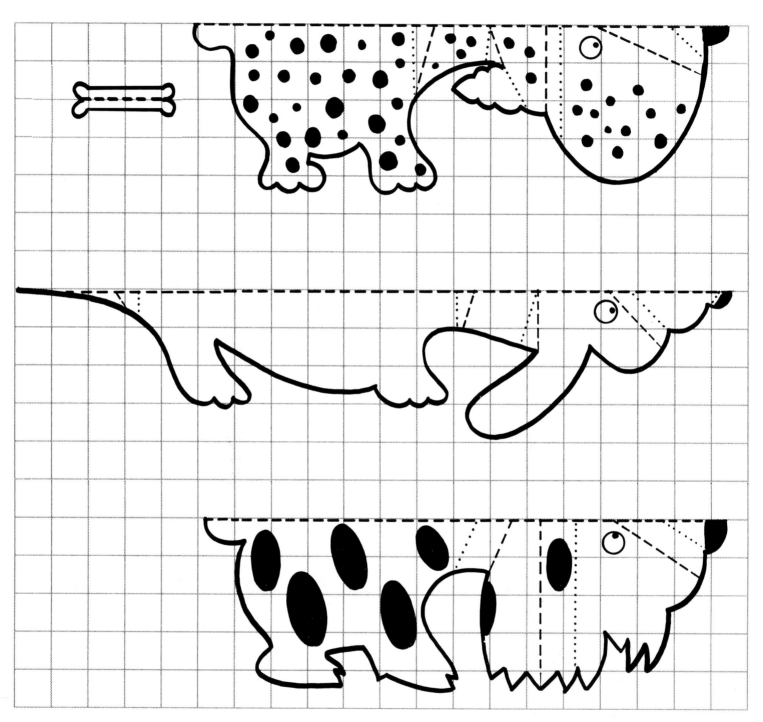

DOGS [16]

The dogs can be cut from thin card or paper. Fold the paper or card double. Transfer the template so that the dotted line matches the fold. Cut out the figure.

For the dogs at the top and bottom of page 20 cut out the mouth through both layers. Fold the dogs along the dotted lines.

Nose, eyes and any spots or stripes can be added with a felt pen. You could also cut out a paper collar and name tag and glue them round the dog's neck.

Cut and fold bones from thin paper.

KENNEL [16]

Cut the kennel out of thin card. Fold the card double. Transfer the template so that the dotted line matches the fold. The kennel itself is shown only as a quarter model on the template. You can see on the illustration below what the kennel should look like when it has been cut out. Make sure that you only cut the opening at the front.

Fold the walls and roof along the dotted lines and assemble as shown.

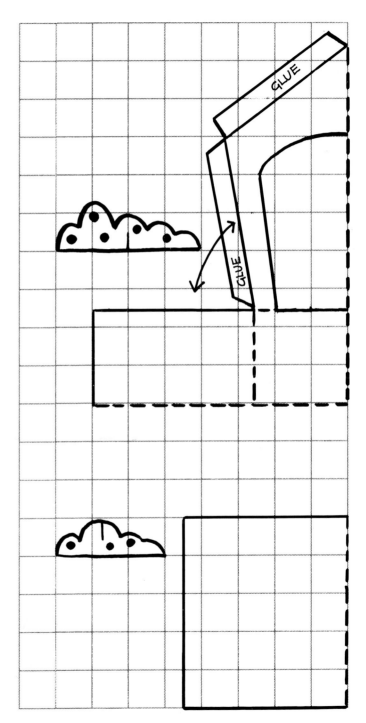

FARM ANIMALS [24] [25]

Cut the horse and the cow from thin card or strong paper. Make the duck and stork from thinner paper. Fold the paper or card double. Transfer the template so that the dotted line matches the fold. Cut out the figure and fold along the dotted lines.

Cow

Cut the body of the cow from brown card or strong paper. Cut the horns from white card and glue them to the ends of the oblong nose. The nose should be curled round and glued to the underside of the cow's head, as shown. Press the horns in place in front of the ears; see illustrations. Cut the udder from pink card or paper and glue it in place. Cut out and glue on the eyes too. The cow could be white with black spots — or the other way around.

Horse

Cut the body of the horse from card or paper. Snip the mane from a piece of paper 7x4 cm. Fold the paper lengthwise and cut almost the whole way through; see the illustration. Glue the mane along the neck. Cut the tail the same way and glue it into position. Cut out and glue on the eyes.

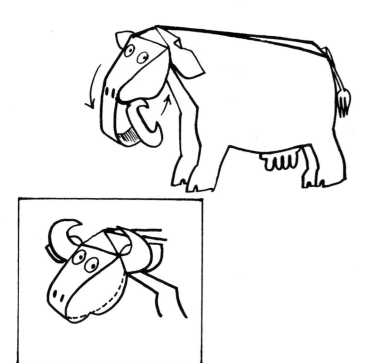

Duck and stork

Cut the duck and stork from paper. Use white paper for the stork. Colour the beak with a red felt pen. Colour the duck's beak too. Draw in the eyes.

Farm animals, pages 22–27.

Hen and cock, page 27

Cow, page 23

Pigs, page 27

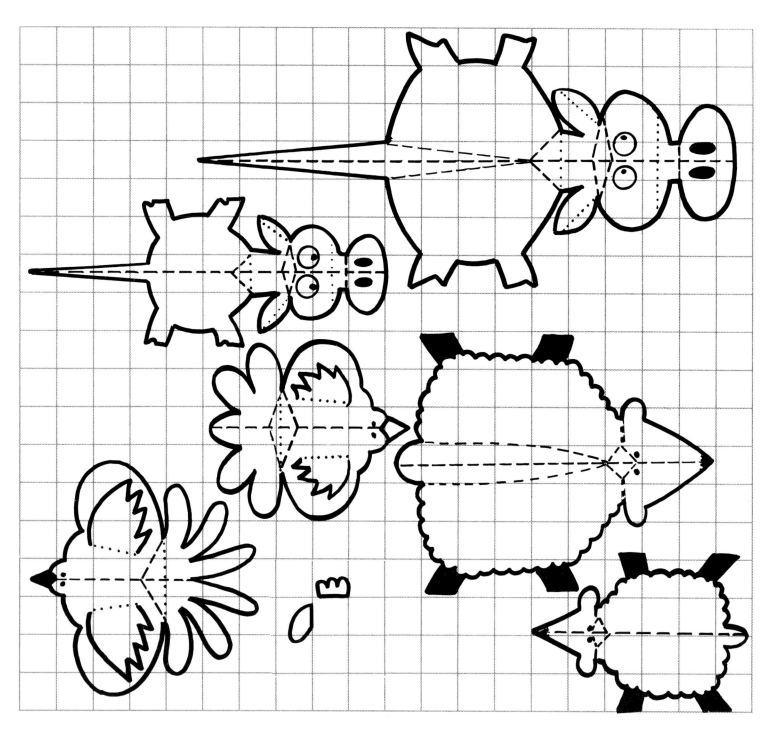

26

FARM ANIMALS [24] [25]

Cut the pig, sheep and lamb from strong paper. Use thinner paper for the hen and cock. Transfer the template to the paper or card. Cut out the figure and fold along the dotted lines.

Pig

Cut the body of the pig from pink paper. Draw in the snout with a pink felt pen. Cut out and glue on the eyes and carefully curl the tail over the edge of a knife or scissor blade.

Sheep and lamb

Cut these from white paper. Draw in the legs and eyes with a black felt pen. If you like you can cut out a little bell and hang it round the neck of the sheep.

Hen and cock

Cut the hen and cock from white, brown or yellow paper. Cut out the wings. Snip the crest and the wattle from red paper and glue it in place. Draw in the eyes with a black felt pen.

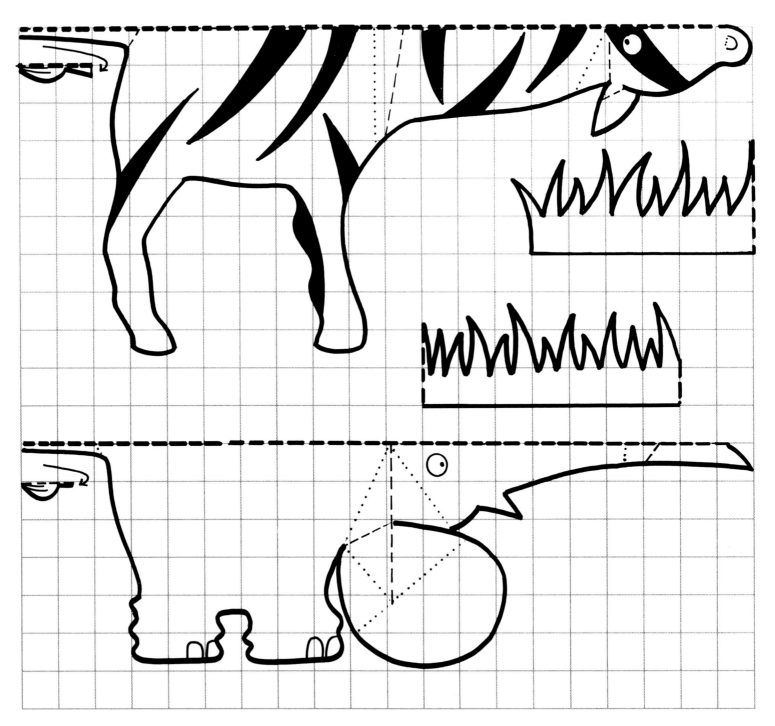

OTHER ANIMALS [32] [33]

Cut the zebra from thin card or strong paper. Cut the elephant from card. Fold the paper or card double. Transfer the templates so that the folds match the dotted lines. Remember to add the tails.

Cut the figures out and fold along the dotted lines.

Zebra

Cut the zebra from white card or paper. Cut out the stripes from black paper and glue them on or simply draw them in with a felt pen.

You can give the animal a mane using the same method as for the horse on page 23. Cut out and glue on the eyes.

Elephant

Cut the elephant from grey card. The template size is suitable for an elephant calf. If you want to make a full-grown elephant you will need to draw the animal on a grid with squares 1.5x1.5 cm; see page 11.

The adult elephant should have tusks cut from white card like the toenails. Cut out and glue on the eyes.

The little tufts of grass can be snipped from green card or paper.

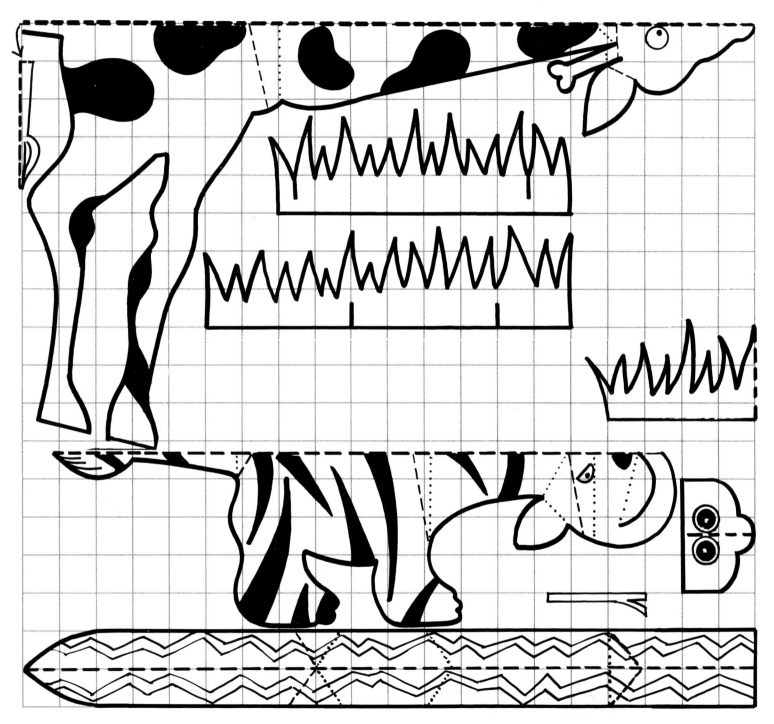

OTHER ANIMALS [32] [33]

Cut the giraffe from card. For the tiger, lion and snake use thin card or strong paper. Fold the paper or card double (but don't do this for the snake as it is a complete template). Transfer the templates so that the dotted lines match the folds. Cut out the figures and fold them along the dotted lines.

Giraffe

Cut the body from yellow card. Snip out the spots from brown paper and glue them on or add them with a felt pen. Cut out and glue on the eyes.

To keep the giraffe standing upright you can glue tufts of grass made from green paper or card to the feet to weigh them down.

Tiger and lion

The tiger and lion are made from the same basic model. Cut the tiger's body from yellow card. The lion's body is brown. Cut the mouth out through both layers. Give the lion whiskers as described in the section on cats on page 15.

Cut the tiger's stripes from orange paper and glue them on or add them with a felt pen. You can also cut teeth from white paper and glue them inside the head so that they can be seen through the open mouth.

Make the lion's mane from orange paper, approximately 10x3 cm. Fold the paper lengthwise and cut it as described in the section on horses on page 23. You can also cut a little tuft for the tail. Glue the mane to the underside of the head all the way round. Draw the nose and cut out and glue the eyes on.

Snake

Cut the snake's body from light green card as shown on page 32. Cut the head and zigzag stripe from dark green card, and the tongue from red paper. Then glue on the zigzag stripe and the head with the tongue in the middle. Glue on the eyes.

31

Zebra, page 29. Giraffe, page 31. Tiger and lion, page 31. Snake, page 31.

Elephants, page 29. Snake, page 31. Palms, page 34.

PALMS [32] [33]

Cut the trunk of the tree from brown card. Use green paper or card for the leaves and yellow for the bananas. Each tree needs two sections for the trunk, two or three bunches of bananas and five or six leaves.

Fold the paper or card double. Transfer the templates so that the fold matches the dotted line. The palm leaves are shown as an entire outline and should be cut in a single layer. Curl the leaves round a pencil or scissor blade. It is easier to curl them before you make the diagonal cuts.

Glue the trunk sections together along the folds as shown in the little illustration. Glue the bunches of bananas and the leaves onto the trunk.

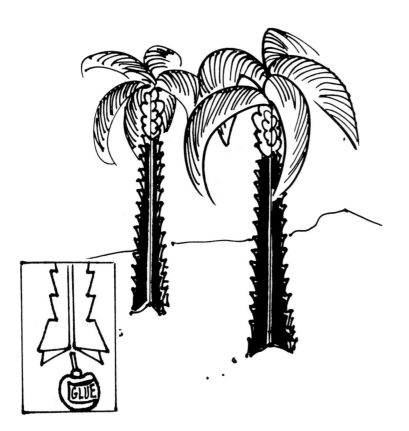

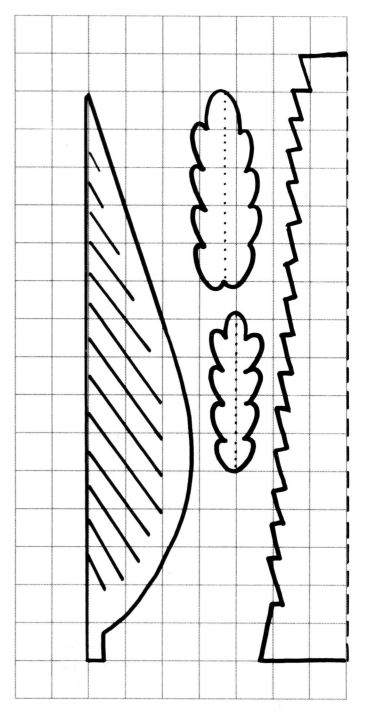

34

FOLDED FLOWERS [40]

Each flower will need a stem, three leaves and a base, all cut from green card. Then cut five petals from card of a contrasting colour. The centre of the flower consists of two parts — one large bloom and one small one, cut from white paper. Cut out the different sections. Fold the petals along the dotted lines as shown in the illustration below:

1. Fold the petal down the middle.
2. Fold the upper curve back.
3. Press the inner petal flat.

Fold the stem and glue it together, making it four-sided. Glue the five petals to the green base. Glue the two white central parts of the flower into the middle. Finally glue the flower and the green leaves to the stem.

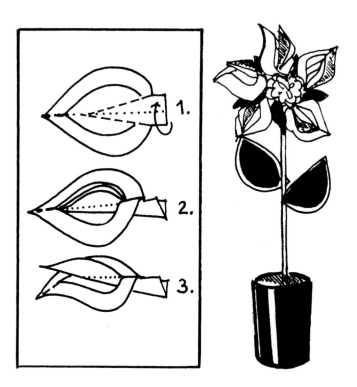

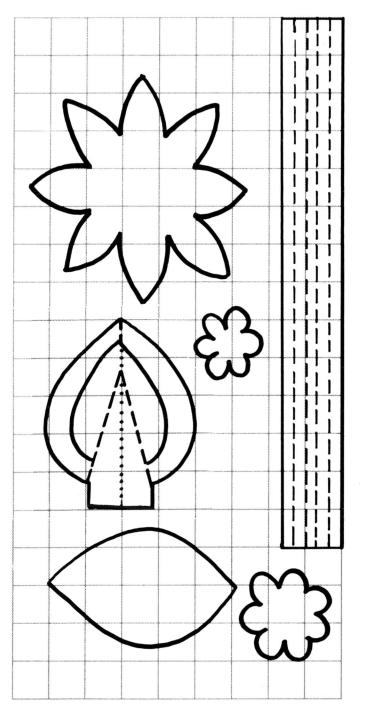

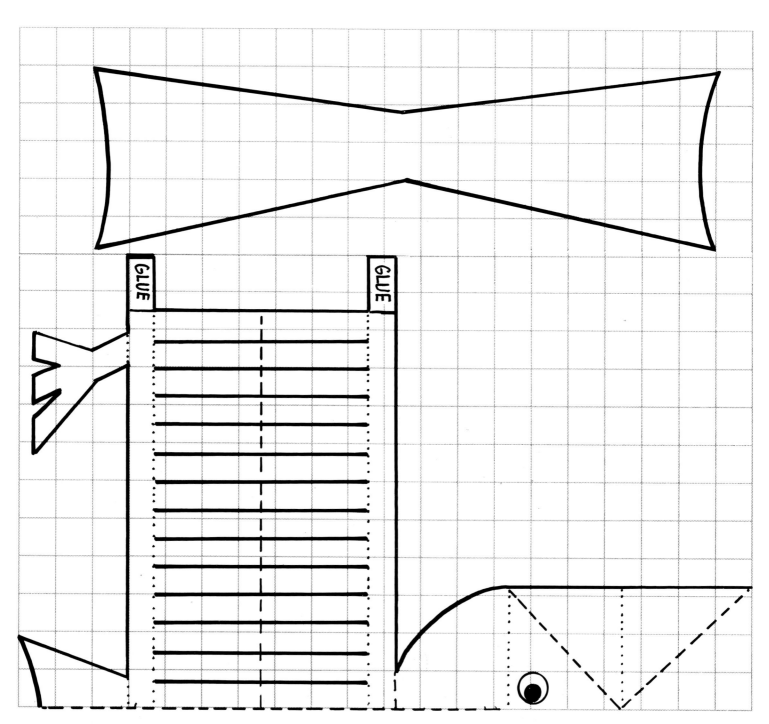

GLUE

GLUE

FANTASY BIRD [41]

Cut the bird from card. The body, head and legs are made in a single piece but the wings are separate. Fold the card double. Transfer the template so that the fold matches the dotted line. Cut the wings through a single layer. Cut out the model. It is best to use a scalpel for the outer strips.

Fold the bird along the dotted lines and glue together to a circular shape. Fold the head into the circle so that it becomes round. Cut out and glue the eyes in place.

Push the wings through the outer strips so that they are level, as shown in the illustration.

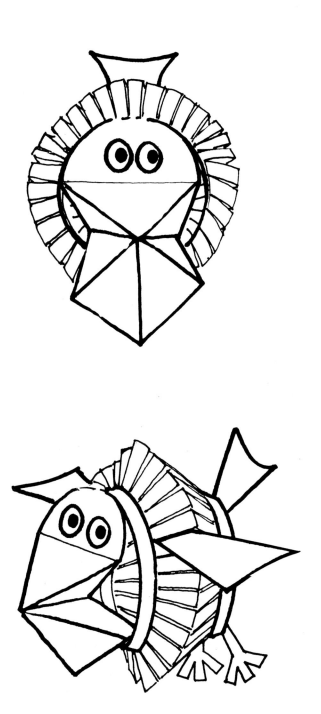

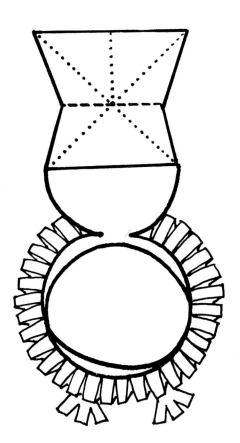

BOUQUET CARD [41]

Cut this from card 16x17 cm and fold across. Use strong paper for the flowers and vase inside the card. Unless stated otherwise use only one piece.

1 = medium green vase (make double).
2 = pale green leaf.
3 = pale green tuft of grass.
4 = dark green leaf.
5 = dark green leaf.
6 = pale green leaf.
7 = blue base flowers (2).
8 = white flowers (2).
9 = pale green grass (make double).
10 = dark green stems (2).
11 = small blue base flowers (2).
12 = small white flowers (2).
13 = pale green base for vase (make double).

Fold piece 1 four times and glue to the card as far as the fold as shown in the illustration below. Glue pieces 2–8 over the upper section of the square as shown. Glue pieces 9–12 to the lower section of the square with the reverse sides facing upwards. Glue small circles into the middle of each flower. Fold the square inwards and glue to piece 13; see illustration on page 41.

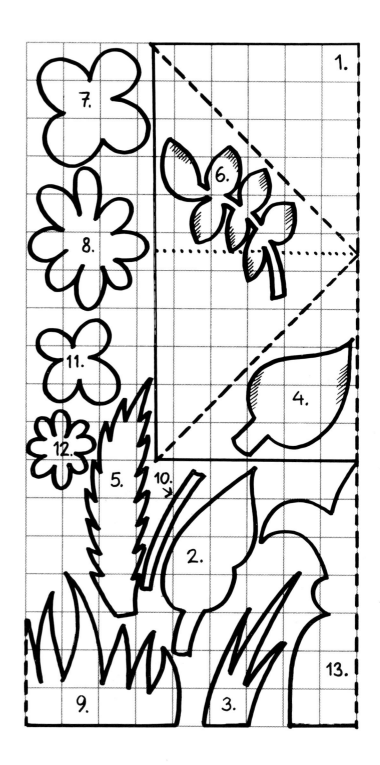

38

TOMATO CARD [41]

This card is a tomato cut from red card. Use paper for the inner sections. The numbers on the template are explained below. The colours correspond to the picture on page 41. Unless otherwise stated use only one piece.

1 = red tomato (make double).
2 = dark green leaf (make double).
3 = orange 'slices' (2).
4 = pink seeds (10).

Fold piece 1. Glue pieces 3–4 as shown below. If you use yellow card and omit the leaves it becomes a honeydew melon instead.

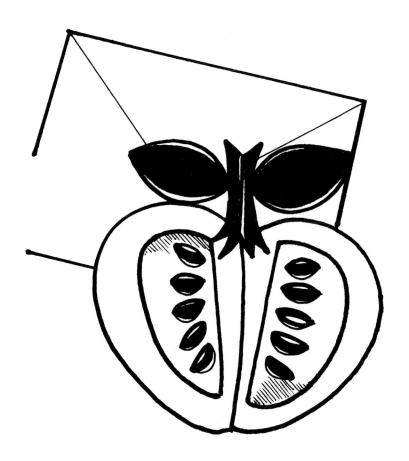

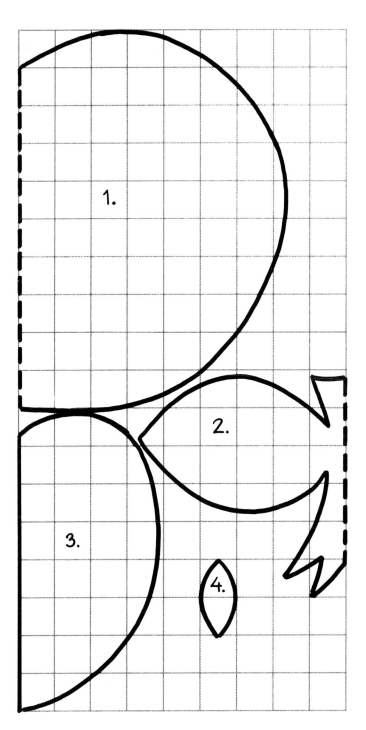

Folded flowers, page 35.

Bouquet card, page 38.

Fantasy bird, page 37.

Cards, pages 39–43.

HEART-SHAPED CARD [41]

This heart shape is cut from card. Use paper for the inner sections. The numbers on the template are explained below. The colours correspond to the picture on page 41. Unless otherwise stated use only one piece.

1 = blue heart (make double).
2 = yellow flower (make double).
3 = pink flower (make double).
4 = small yellow flower (make double).
5 = pink 'stamens' (make double).
6 = pale green and dark green ribbons (2 in all).
7 = pale green leaves (2).

Fold piece 1 and glue pieces 5–7; see positions on the upper drawing. Glue pieces 2–4 on top. You can also vary the card. For example, see the red heart-shaped card illustrated on page 41.

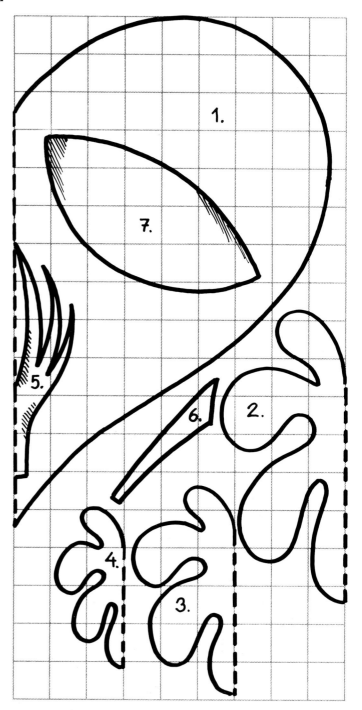

FLOWER CARD AND BEAR CARD [41]

Cut these from card but use paper for the inner sections. The numbers on the template are explained below. The colours correspond to the picture on page 41. Unless otherwise stated use only one piece.

Flower card
1a = dark green leaves (make double).
2a = pink flower (make double).
3a = pink flower (make double).
4a = pale green leaves (2).

Fold piece 1a and glue on pieces 2a–4a as shown in the illustration below.

Bear card
1b = pink head of bear.
2b = pink ears (2).
3b = pink eyes.
4b = green flower stem.
5b = yellow flower.

Fold piece 1b and glue on pieces 2b–5b as shown in the illustration. Draw in the mouth, eyes and nose with a black felt pen. Glue the head to both sides of the card so that it folds outwards when you open the card.

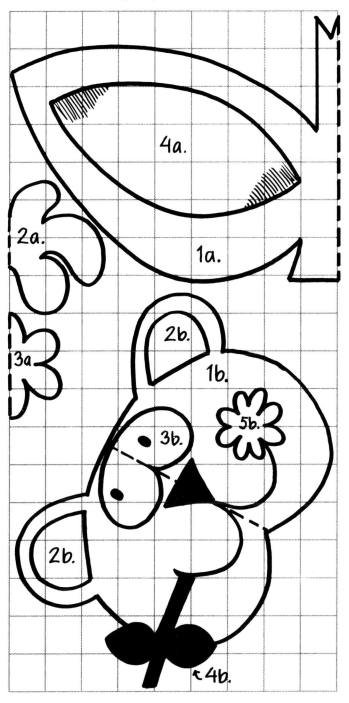

1.

2.

3.

4.

5.

6.

7.

8.

44

HARES [48] [49]

You can use the hares in this section either as table cards on in chains. The numbers on the template are explained below. The colours correspond to the pictures on pages 48 and 49. Unless otherwise stated use only one piece. Cut all sections from card.

Hare chains

The chain could consist, for example, of four hares folded from thin brown card, 48x18 cm. Fold accordion-style in four layers, 12x18 cm. If you do not have large pieces of card you could reduce the size of the hares. You could also glue several chains together to make a long one. Transfer the template to the top section of card and cut out the hare through all layers. The hares should 'hold hands' and must not be cut free. Cut a hole for the mouth and glue the teeth on the inside as shown in the illustration. All the hares should have bow-ties; see template number 8.

Table cards

You can cut the table cards in, for example, yellow or mauve as shown in the picture on page 48.

Yellow hare:

1 = yellow body.	3 = mauve name board.
2 = white teeth.	4 = mauve hat.

Cut a hole for the mouth and glue the teeth on the inside as shown in the illustration. Press the name board down into the slits in the paws. Glue on the hat. Draw in the nose and eyes.

Mauve hare:
1 = mauve body.
2 = white teeth.
3 = green name board.
5 = green hat.
6 = yellow flower with white centre.
7 = green stem.

Cut a hole for the mouth and glue on the teeth as shown. Attach the name board as described above. Glue on the hat and flower. Draw in the nose and eyes.

EGG CHAINS [48]

Eggshell chains

Cut the chain from white card, for example, 36x5 cm. Fold the card accordion-style in four layers, 9x5 cm. Transfer the doubled eggshells to the top section of card and cut out through all layers. The ends of the eggshells should be joined and must not be cut free. Attach the chicks to the shells; see page 47.

Egg cup chains

Make this chain from blue card, for example, 30x5 cm. Fold accordion-style in six layers, 5x5 cm. Transfer the egg cup to the top section of card and cut out through all layers. The corners of the egg cups should be joined and must not be cut free. Cut the border at the bottom from yellow paper and glue it to the egg cups. Cut three eggshells and three egg halves from white card. Glue the eggs alternately to the back of the cups as shown in the illustration. Attach the chicks to the shells; see page 47.

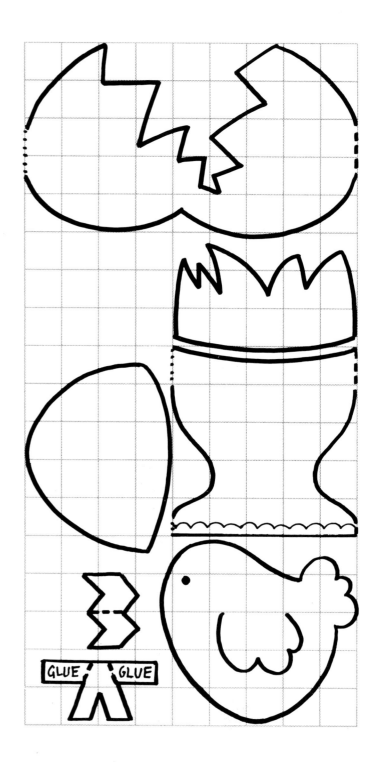

GLUE GLUE

CHICKS [48]

The chicks can be attached with the help of their wings, for example, to branches. You could also join them to various chains; see page 46 where you will also find the templates. Cut the chicks from yellow card. Snip the wings free and bend them outwards slightly. Cut the beak from red card, fold and glue as shown.

Chicks with feet

To make a chick with feet you need two template sections. Glue the two chicks together as shown in the illustration. Glue the feet by bending the two glued ends upwards. See also the illustration on page 51.

FLOWER CHAINS [48]

The numbers on the template are: 1 = blades of grass, drawn onto green card folded as shown on page 45; it should measure 5x6 cm. 2 = the leaves, which are glued to the stems. 3 and 4 = the flowers, which are glued on top of each other. They should be glued to the stems, as should flowers 5 and 6.

Hare table cards, page 45.

Chicks, p 47. Flower chain, p 47.

Egg chains, page 46.

48

Hare chain, page 45.

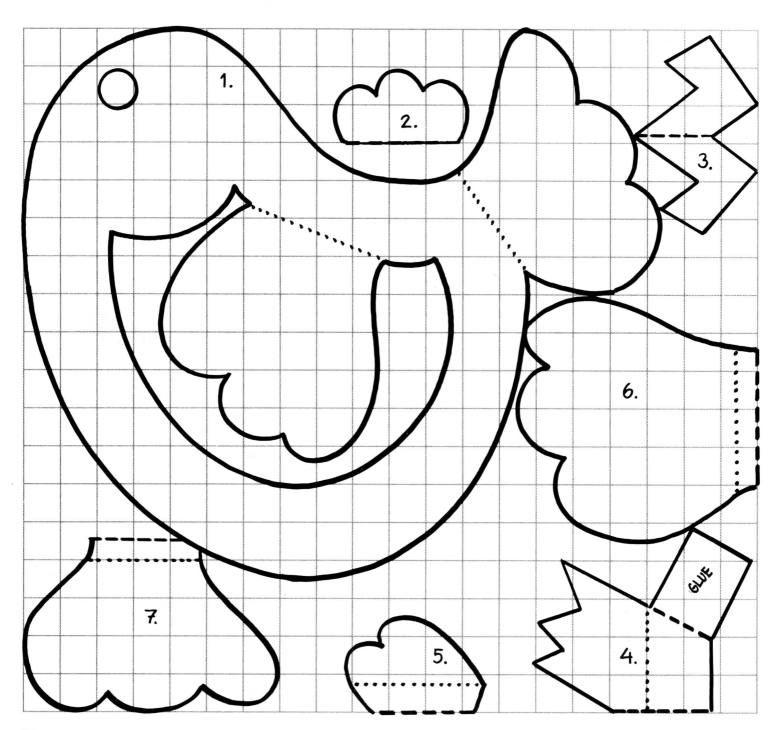

1.

2.

3.

4.

5.

6.

7.

GLUE

BROWN HEN [56]

The hen is made double so that it will stand up. The numbers on the template are explained below. The colours correspond to the picture on page 56. Unless otherwise stated use only one piece. Cut all sections from card.

1 = brown body sections (2).
2 = red crest.
3 = red beak.
4 = red feet (make double).
5 = red wattle (make double).
6 = brown wings (make double).
7 = brown tail feather (make double).

Glue the wattle, crest, doubled wings and doubled tail feather to one body section as shown below. Glue the other body section along the head and back. Glue the beak and feet as shown in the illustrations. Fold the wings and tail feathers outwards.

WHITE HEN [56]

Make the white hen in the same way as the brown hen on page 51. The numbers on the template are explained below. Unless otherwise stated use only one piece. Cut all sections from card.

1 = white body sections (2).
2 = red crest.
3 = red wattle.
4 = red feet.
5 = red beak.
6 = brown tail feather.
7 = brown wings.

Lay the body sections on top of each other. Place the wattle and crest between them. Glue the head and back together. Glue the wings and tail feathers along the dotted lines. Glue the beak and feet as shown in the illustrations on page 51.

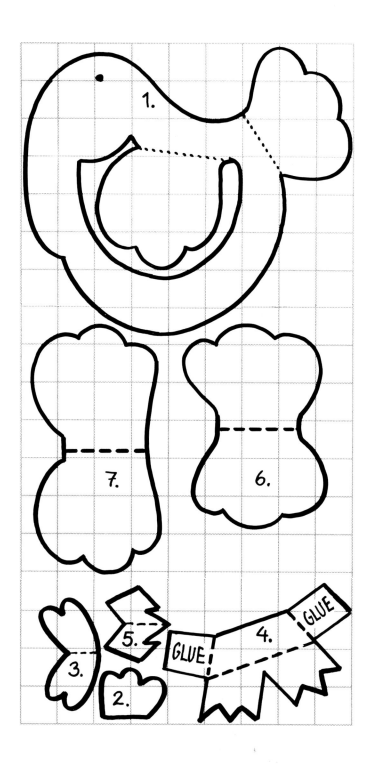

52

FLUFFY CHICK [57]

The fluffy yellow chick is made from two pieces in the same way as the other models described. Cut all sections from card. Use two body sections, glued together along the head, back and tail. Glue the feet and beak as shown on page 51.

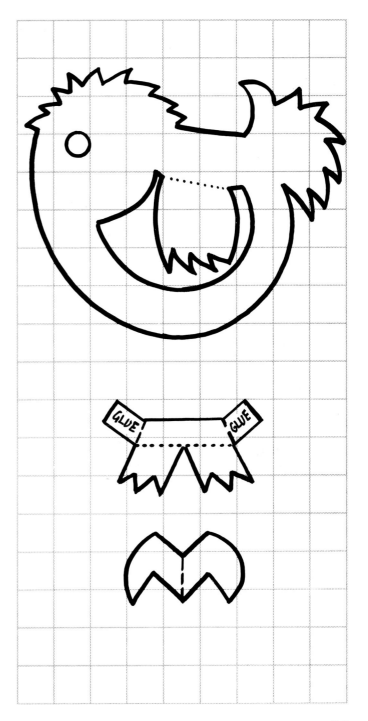

BLUEBIRD [57]

The bluebird can, of course, be cut out in any colour. It is very similar to the designs already described but it has no feet and hangs on a thread.

Use two bodies for each bird and glue them together along the head, back and tail. Don't forget to place a piece of thread in between for hanging. Glue the wings between the dotted lines as shown in the drawing. The beak should also be glued on.

SILHOUETTES [57]

Cut or trim the small silhouettes from a single colour piece of card. If you make the big silhouette make sure you cut the beaks and bow in a matching colour and glue them on. If the model is to hang in a window, cut the bow and beaks double and glue them on both sides so that there is no reverse side.

Chicks, page 47. Brown hen, page 51. White hen, page 52.

Bluebirds, page 54.

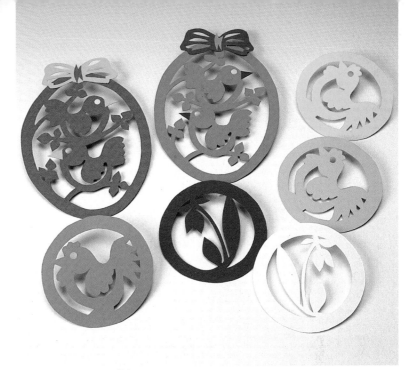

Silhouettes, page 54.

Fluffy chicks, page 53.

57

SPRING TREES [64]

Cut the trees from card. For each tree you will need two template sections (laid double). As you can see from the template the trees should be extended at the bottom. Glue or staple the trees along the fold as shown in the illustration. You can decorate them with leaves or birds. If you choose leaves you should use around 100 and they should be cut in a contrasting colour. The birds should be white with red beaks and black eyes. You should use 20–25 birds for each tree. If you like you can modify the tree shown in the picture on page 49.

BIRD CHAINS [64]

Make the chains from card. Cut or fold them as described on page 45. The dimensions depend on the size of the template. You can use the chains as an Easter decoration or on a window-sill.

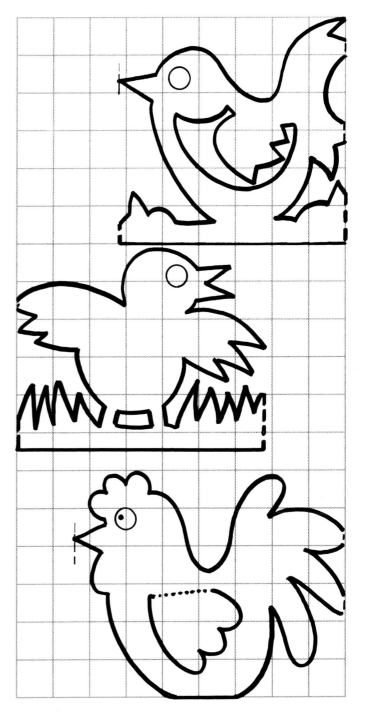

EASTER CARDS [64]

The backing should be cut from yellow card, about 12x20 cm, and folded across. Cut the other parts from card as well. Use two doubled white hens. Draw the crest, beak and wattle on the four heads with a red felt pen. Two of the heads should have drawings on both sides. The eyes should be black. Glue one pair of hens into the middle of the card along the fold. Glue the other pair on top; see the illustration. You can also staple in two flowers and two tufts of grass (laid double) in contrasting shades of colour.

60

SHEEP [64]

Cut the big sheep from white card and fold it along the dotted line. The ears should be cut from pink paper and the eyes from blue. Draw the hoofs, nose and pupils in the eyes black. Use a cotton wool ball for the tail.

Pairs of sheep

Glue the sheep together, nose to nose. The body (see the dotted line) should be cut from brown card. Cut the fleece out of white card. The eyes should be blue and the grass and flowers cut from green, yellow and blue card. Glue the sheep together in pairs with a bouquet of flowers between their noses as shown in the illustration. Draw the noses and eyes in black. Glue the sheep to a patch of grass made from green card. This will make it easier for them to stand.

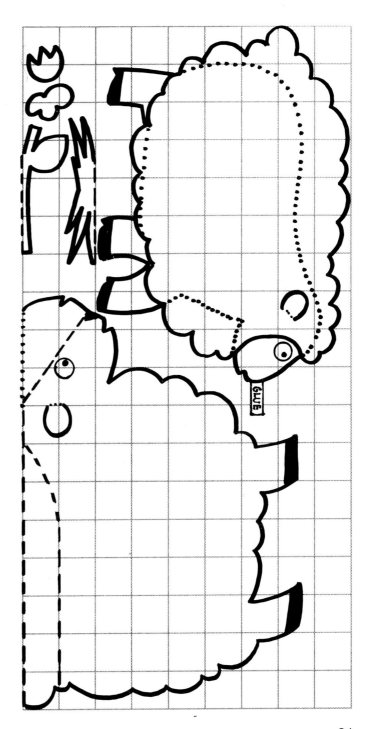

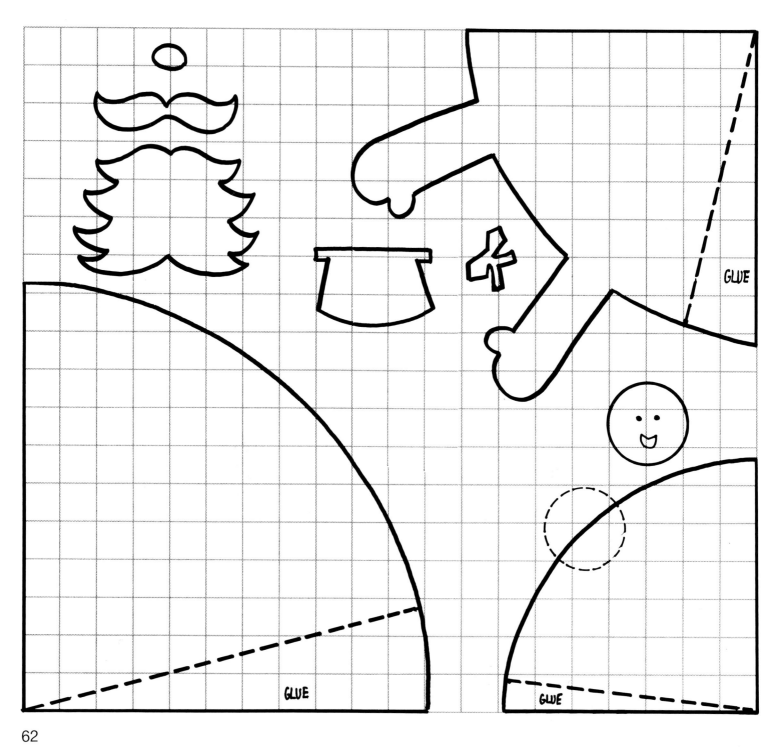

GLUE

GLUE

GLUE

CONE GNOMES [65]

Make Daddy Gnome and Mummy Gnome from strong paper cones. Use three cones for each model. You can vary the colours — use grey and red, for example — to make the trolls different.

The templates are suitable for medium-sized figures but you can obviously make them larger or smaller. The biggest cone is for the bottom section of the body. The next largest cone is for the upper body and arms. The smallest cone is for the cap. Cut a white border and tassel for the cap.

Draw the eyes on the face and glue this to the inside of the cap; see illustration. Daddy Gnome should have a beard and red nose. Mummy Gnome should have a red mouth and white hair cut from a frilly strip. She should also have an apron and a bow glued to the bottom cone. Place the cones over each other as shown.

Sheep, page 61.

Spring trees, p 58. Easter cards p 60. Chicks p 47.

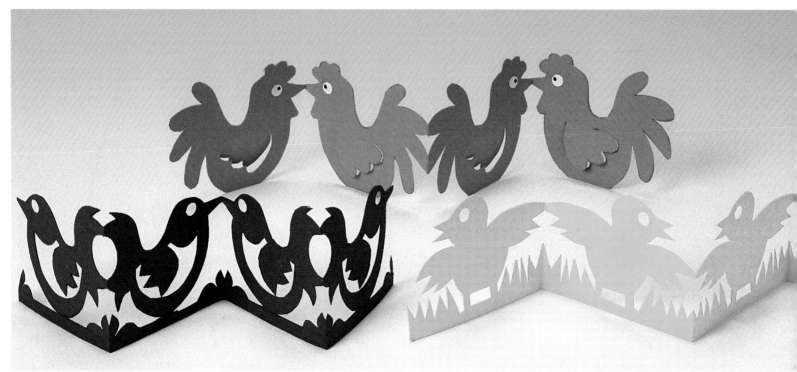

Bird chains, page 59.

64

Cone gnomes, page 63. Christmas tree, page 67.

CHRISTMAS TREE DECORATIONS [73]

All the templates in this section are halves and should therefore be doubled. You will see that the paired templates have the same basic outline but the cut-outs inside are different. On some models the inside section is cut out completely. On others the surrounding line is cut free so that the shape can be folded back; see illustration.

Use two whole templates for each model and staple or glue them together. You can glue a star on top of the little Christmas tree. Attach a thread to each model to hang it up.

CHRISTMAS TREE [65]

Cut the Christmas tree from green card. You will need two complete template sections (laid double) for each tree. Fold the inner 'points' outwards. Glue or staple the trees together and decorate them with about 32 lights made from white and yellow paper. Add about 20 red hearts and a star at the top.

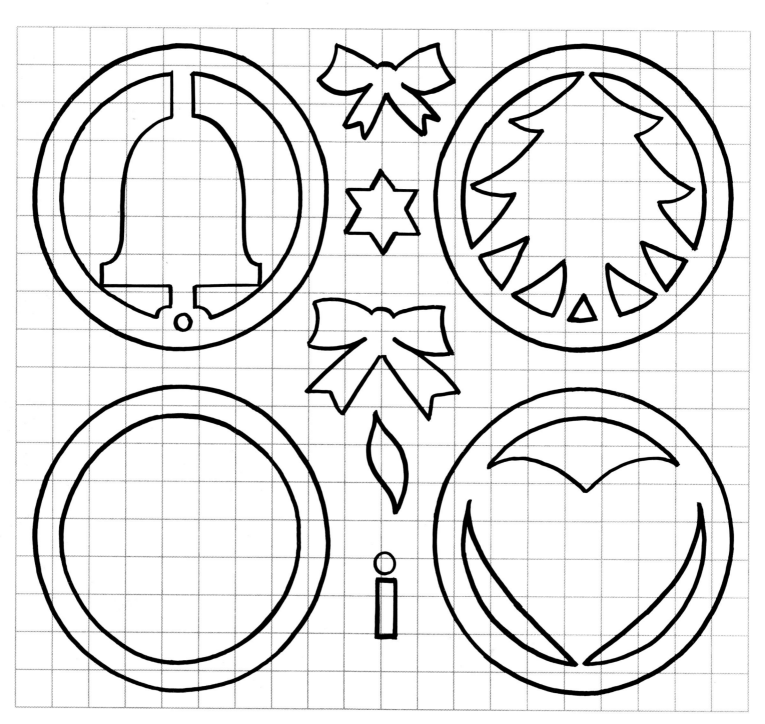

CHRISTMAS WREATHS [72]

Cut the wreaths from red, green, white and yellow card. You can combine the different models. The picture on page 72 shows some of the ways you can decorate the wreaths. The Christmas bell wreath is cut from red card with a gold base and a green bow on top. The middle part of the hammer is green. The entwined wreath is green with a red band around it. The Christmas tree wreath is green with a gold base. Decorate the tree with white lights and a red star. The heart wreath is red with a green bow. The base of the heart is gold. The Advent wreath is green with a red band, bows and white candles.

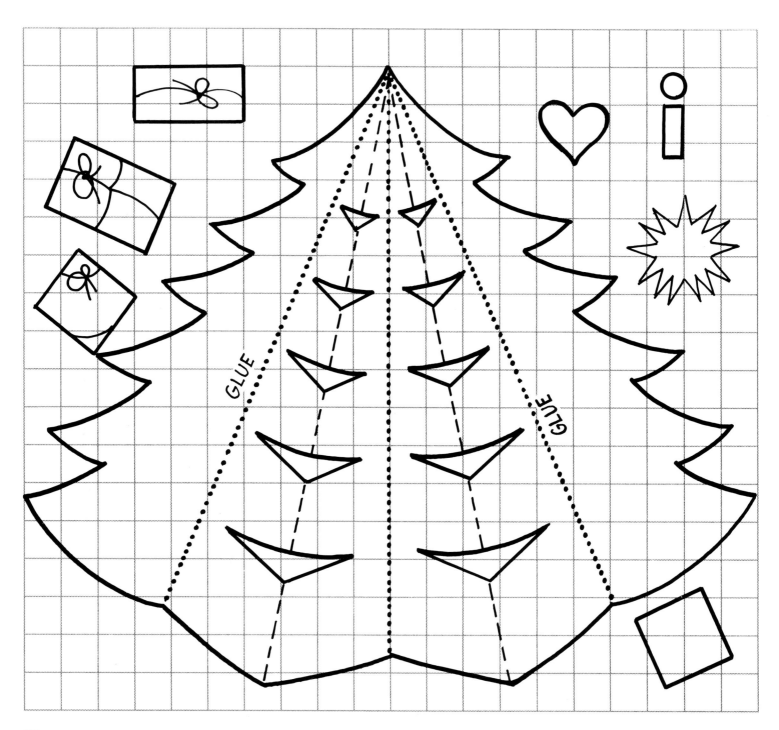

CHRISTMAS CARDS [72]

Cut each one from green card, 18x21 cm, and fold it lengthwise. Cut and fold the Christmas tree from green paper. Glue the tree as shown in the illustration. It is important to make sure that the tree folds correctly when the card closes. For decoration use about 10 candles made from white and yellow paper, a white star and 8–10 gold hearts. Cut about 10 Christmas parcels from coloured paper and glue them underneath the tree. Draw ribbons and bows on them.

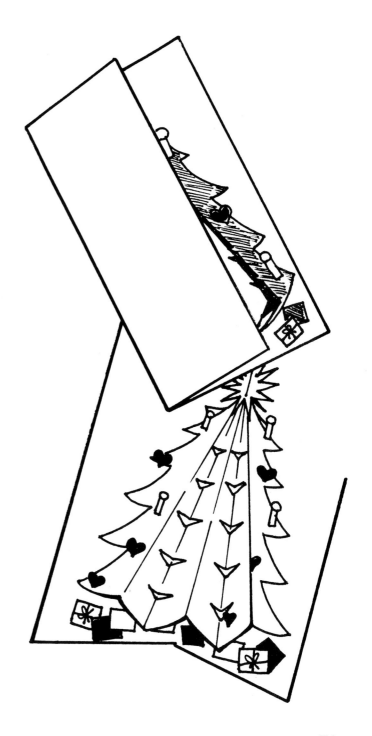

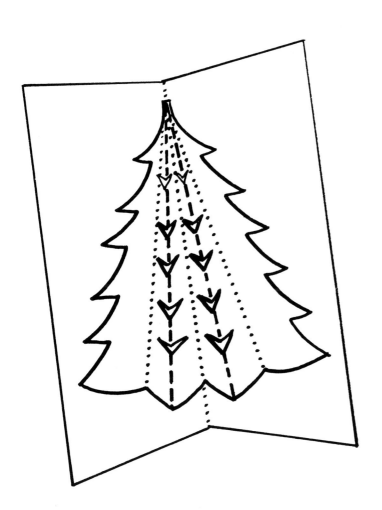

Christmas wreaths, page 68. Christmas cards, page 71.

Flying angels, page 76.

Orchestra of angels, page 75.

Christmas tree decorations, page 66. Gnomes in a ring, page 77.

ORCHESTRA OF ANGELS [73]

Cut each angel from a single piece of white card. Place the two half-template sections end to end as shown in the illustration. When you transfer the template the card should be doubled. Make sure that the wing slots are cut opposite each other so that they can be pressed together; see the illustration.

Cut the face from skin-coloured paper and glue it to the model. The eyelids should be open. Glue a gold heart underneath the head. Fold the top half of the model back, and push the arms through the two slits at the front. Press the wings together and fold the upper section of the head down as shown to give the top a pleated effect. Cut the hair from gold foil and push it down behind the head.

FLYING ANGEL [73]

Cut and fold the body of each angel from white card (laid double). Cut the face from skin-coloured paper and glue it in position. Make sure that the eyelids are open when you glue the head. The mouth should be red. Cut the wings from gold foil.

If you wish you can glue red paper to the reverse side; see the picture on page 73. Glue the wings to the back as shown in the illustration. Curl the arms round over a scissor blade so that they bend up or down.

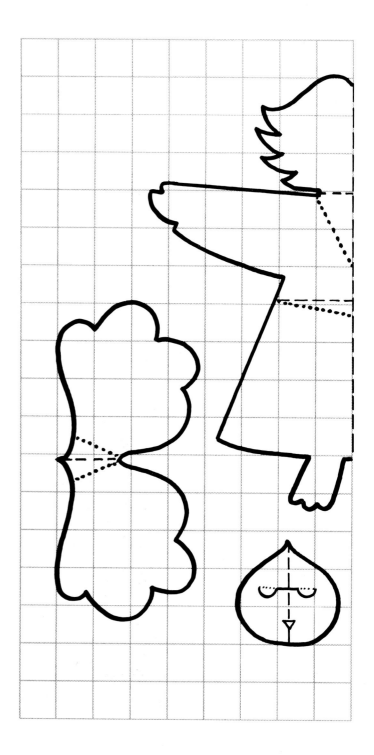

GNOMES IN A RING [73]

The gnomes, which are dancing round in a ring, can be cut from red card using the method outlined on page 45. When you fold the card it should measure 7x12 cm. Cut the other sections from paper. The tassels on the hats should be white, and the faces skin-coloured. Draw the eyes on the faces.

As you can see from the illustration below, each figure is either a man-gnome or a woman-gnome. The man-gnome has a white beard and a red nose. The woman-gnome has a white apron and bow, and a red mouth.